Chasing the
Perfect Moment

Chasing the Perfect Moment

Ginny Brown

Ginny Brown, C.L.C., LCHW
15019 Miss Ellie Drive
San Antonio, Texas 78247
www.chasingtheperfectmoment.com

Editing and Book Layout ©2018 Night Owl Services

Ordering Information:
Quantity sales. Special discounts are available on quantity purchases by corporations, associations, and others. For details, contact the publisher at the address above.

Chasing the Perfect Moment/Ginny Brown. -- 1st ed.
ISBN 978-0-692-05480-2

Dedication

To my beautiful husband, Mike Brown,
who still—even in death—continues to love and
encourage me.

Michael Hayes Brown

02/19/2017

Contents

The Journey

One day you finally knew
what you had to do, and began,
though the voices around you
kept shouting
their bad advice,
though the whole house
began to tremble
and you felt the old tug
at your ankles.
"Mend my life!"
each voice cried.
But you didn't stop.
You knew what you had to do,
though the wind pried
with its stiff fingers
at the very foundations,

though their melancholy
was terrible.
It was already late
enough, and a wild night
and the road full of fallen
branches and stones.
But, little by little,
as you left their voices behind,
the stars began to burn
through the sheets of clouds,
and there was a new voice
which you slowly
recognized as your own,
that kept you company
as you strode deeper and deeper
into the world,
determined to do
the only thing you could do,
determined to save
the only life you could save.

~Mary Oliver

Introduction

"Unless you are prepared to give up something valuable you will never be able to truly change at all, because you'll be forever in the control of things you can't give up."

~Andy Law

Without sounding too clichéd, how many "little white picket fences" do we build each day? Stories that make us feel good or safe. Each slat inserted around us, constructing what we think will make us happy and secure within it. How many of these "feel-good" moments have we chased and can't let go of because they make us feel comfortable in a world in which we feel uncomfortable or dissatisfied? Tugging and seducing, lulling us into a false sense of security. If we get stuck in these moments too long they can compromise the inner voice that calls to us, the authenticity that is screaming behind the scenes for us to live our life genuinely. While there is always a place for beautiful memories, those special moments that sincerely do warm our hearts, they are not a substitute to hide behind from the realities of life.

Vice versa, how many moments do we run from? Our minds quickly changing gears like a finger touched to a hot iron, when unpleasant moments or memories rear their ugly little heads? We don't want to think about them.

Trapped in emotional residuals from our growing pains, joys, hurts, and frustrations throughout our many life experiences, many of us lie in pieces. We wait for something or someone to reassemble us into complete beings, trying to make the pieces of our life fit into a world that's not working anymore.

While we run our life's course, chase our tails, and pretend to be something we are not, through it all like a loyal companion and friend, our genuine self waits for our return. It calls to us throughout our lives and in the many messes we get ourselves into.

Struggling with big, square, and immovable-box ways of thinking, with hard edges that poke and prod us with *shoulds* and *should-nots*, learned behaviors, and societal norms, most of us live our life stuck in these thought processes. Resisting the natural flow of things, we struggle, selectively grasping those things we reason will bring happiness and relevance into our lives.

If we dare, however, to step outside the box, this flow waits to free us from being stifled by the mental constructs of fear, insecurity, and limited thinking. Like a blank canvas where anything is possible, this creative force waits for us to pick up our crayons and draw, our potential and purpose ready to be discovered.

"Chasing the Perfect Moment" will help to you to make this discovery by asking questions and looking at life in a creative and inspirational way, and is designed to help you gain new perspective based on the following principles:

- Living a successful life is living the **real** you.
- Change is **moving forward.**
- **Leaving** old moments behind, as perfect or imperfect as they may be, and creating and living in **new moments,** starting with now.
- Finding out and accepting **who you are.**

To be genuine takes courage. Are you ready to throw back the covers, expose old belief systems, and see what's not working anymore? What does carving out a life that works for you look like?

Together we will chase our perfect moments until we catch them, truly look at them, find the sacred pieces of us within, and let go of the rest. With an open mind and heart, we will move forward with courage to examine, explore, re-evaluate, and look at life from different perspectives.

I believe there is an imaginary line that runs parallel between us and the childhoods that we leave behind, those magical places where many of us spent days daydreaming about our future potential and hope for a better world. Throughout our lives, the line never goes away but ebbs and flows as we experience our day to day living. I invite you to look at your own imaginary line. Is it dividing you from the hope and childlike wonder now cocooned in your heart because you *grew up*? This book asks this and many more questions in the hope that you use it as a tool to guide, transform, and move you in ways that help you discover, reconnect, and reinvent a more colorful and genuine life.

> "There is something in every one of you that waits and listens for the sound of the genuine in yourself. It is the only true guide you will ever have. And if you cannot hear it, you will all of your life spend your days on the ends of strings that somebody else pulls."
>
> ~Howard Thurman, based on excerpts from his Baccalaureate Address at Spelman College, (4 May 1980)

CHAPTER ONE

The First Moment

"There must be always remaining in every life, some place for the singing of angels, some place for that which in itself is breathless and beautiful."

~Howard Thurman

Caroline Myss, in her book, *Sacred Contracts*, wrote that the first stage of our Sacred Contract, or calling in life, is contact: "A divine filled moment of connection that occurs between you and your creator." It is in this moment that we get to *touch the heavens* and bring back a piece of it with us. The *first moment* is like a place not of this Earth that calls to us at some time in our life through special moments, people, or places that we connect with and hold most sacred. It is this moment that inspires the greatest of paintings, books, and songs when the author, painter, or singer takes us, if only briefly, back to a proverbial sense of *home*. It is this first moment, suspended in time and anchored by memory, that echoes to us throughout our life. Reaching to us through every thread of authenticity, it waits for us to answer.

If, and when, we do answer this profound moment, that is when we find ourselves suddenly thrust into the possibility-driven tango we call life. Fulfilled as though there is a rush of stars aligning brightly and lighting the way, signaling for our journey to begin, it is the "aha" moment of divine familiarity that we seek through our own private portals, or as Paul Coelho writes in his book, *The Alchemist*, "intuition is really a sudden immersion of the soul into the universal current of life, where the histories of all people are connected." Never separate from this sacred connection, we do, however, short circuit occasionally, unfortunately forgetting how to plug back in.

When I was a little girl, my Uncle Oscar would tell me, in his thick German accent, "Little Ginny, the moon is made of green cheese!" Determined to see this green cheese, I spent many an endless night on our porch swing gazing at the moon and wondering about my uncle's words. Finally, I decided that my uncle was not only trying to stretch my imagination and rouse my curiosity, but also teaching me how to see and appreciate something so magnificent. He shared his own appreciation with me for this big, white (or green, depending on how you look at it) orb that even today nestles in the stars and glows above me, representing a kind of mysterious power that fills me with wonder each time I see it. Gazing upon the moon, I can still feel those long-ago sensations of being lifted above my ordinary world, to be safely and lovingly delivered into the imaginary arms of something so much greater than my small surroundings. Each nightly experience spoke to my heart, whispering future dreams and filling me with renewed hope. Resilience grew where there was once insecurity, and new determination blossomed. It was my first connection to divinity and it is that heartfelt conduit that remains as the precious jewel, the *magic* that I protect at all costs as my heirloom of faith. It is the realness in my life; it is my portal to God.

God or Green Cheese?

> "Every visible and invisible creature is an appearance of God."
>
> ~John Scotus Erigena

As a child, peering through the open portal to this creative intelligence—or God—was so much easier. God did not have a face yet. This magnificent creative force was a sudden rainstorm, a minuscule bug, a loving smile and even the "green cheese" of the moon. Life was an array of magic that came through intuition and simple curiosity. Every color, flower, and person spoke through this divine intelligence. In every picture I drew, every poem I wrote, every star I wished upon, there it was, this God that was at home in me.

To be as a child means escaping the hardcore beliefs, judgments, and opinions that as an adult, settle in and divide us rather than unite us with the present moment. If we can understand that we are not separated by these walls, using this child heart to navigate ourselves from a new perspective and asking, "Where do I go from here?" and "What is it I truly want from my life?" we might find that the answers are closer than we think.

Opening ourselves to this connection, we rediscover creativity and imagination, exposing ourselves to new opportunities. Graced with enchantment and connected to the beauty in all things, the child heart never forgets the wonder and the innocence to know God when it sees it and to carve a genuine life that reflects it.

As I open my own mind and heart, disabling defenses and inflexibilities, I am reminded that a reasoning mind alone is not always the answer.

Behind the Veils

"... for the past 33 years, I have looked in the mirror every morning and asked myself: 'If today were the last day of my life, would I want to do what I am about to do today?' And whenever the answer has been 'No' for too many days in a row, I know I need to change something."

~Steve Jobs, Stanford University commencement address (12 June 2005)

Our life is about purpose and creating and following our own personal and individual genuine path. That can only be the right one for us. If we follow a different well-worn road we can get stuck by an unhealthy amount of logic and subdued by habitual paths or patterns that take us nowhere.

Whether it's the last day of your life or the first day of the rest of your life, you have to live life in a way that honors you, that honors who you are. Ask yourself if you really identify with what you are doing or if you are just going through the motions. Once you choose to answer that genuine call and the layers of self-doubt and constricting veils are pulled back, you can jump off the hamster wheel and watch your small world expand.

In her book, *Return to Love*, Marianne Williamson wrote, "Your playing small does not serve the world." We do not do anyone any favors by *hiding our light* and pretending to be *smaller than we are*. And, once the universe sees your beacon bravely and brightly lit, it will answer in ways you didn't dream were possible.

Until the "tap, tap, tap" of our divine call is answered and our spirituality freed, we will never recognize our true potential. Our creative energies, until now, have been shelved in the dust as our soul cries out an invitation for us to live an authentic and amazing life, a life that we are happy to wake up to each day.

Whatever whispers to you, whatever makes your heart sing, whatever special place you call home, is still there—waiting.

> "If ever there is tomorrow when we're not together…there is something you must always remember. You are braver than you believe, stronger than you seem, and smarter than you think. But the most important thing is, even if we're apart…I'll always be with you."
>
> ~Carter Crocker and Karl Geurs, *Pooh's Grand Adventure: The Search for Christopher Robin*

First chapter questions:

What does your first moment feel, look, or sound like?

From where does it call to you?

How do you plug into it?

CHAPTER TWO

The Perfect Moment

"You can clutch the past so tightly to
your chest that it leaves your arms too full
to embrace the present."

~Jan Glidewell

A friend of mine, Doris, and myself continu-
ally joke about our latest "perfect moments."
When one of us describes a moment for the
other that was anything less than perfect, we laugh
and joke about how this or that was NOT a perfect
moment! It's our way of finding humor in some of
life's more challenging moments. But in all honesty,
if we look closely, all moments are perfect in their
insane, terrifying, funny, sad, humorous, life-shatter-
ing and -defining ways. They are who we are, who we
have become, and what the extent of our life will be,
depending on how we decide to peer through these
experiences. Their mind-altering ways are powerful

and meaningful. If the first moment, the time we felt connected, were not so important, why do we spend the rest of our lives searching and chasing after it in one form or another?

That one perfect moment can cradle us in its arms like a favorite overstuffed armchair so cozy we never want to leave. It becomes a cherished memory that can play over and over. If left unchecked, this memory can serve as a safe haven, falsely protecting us from a reality that in comparison seems like a cold cruel world. Rather than embrace reality, it becomes easier to follow around that last perfect moment like a lovesick puppy absorbed in the feel-good memory of it. A perfect moment, as lovely and as enticing as it may be, can be just as limiting as being caught up in unwelcome moments. If we are trapped by emotion and too busy chasing our perfect moment, how does reality stand a chance to offer us something greater?

Framing the Moment

"It is that perfect moment when we believe all of us and all around us are in harmony. Only children know it, and the clouds and the sea."

~Anita Nair, *The Lilac House*

If you could frame one perfect moment, event, or time from the past, what would that moment be? The one moment or place suspended in time that you felt loved, safe, and happier than you have ever felt before? A moment that to this day connects or acts as your portal to that first moment or connection?

My perfect moment, framed by the savory smells and delightful sounds of Christmas in my childhood, never fails to arouse my feelings of *home*. A moment that transcends time, I can still smell the intoxicating and heavenly aroma of warm chocolate baking in our oven, its velvet warmth filling my nostrils and tickling my senses from head to toe. Excited and grinning from ear-to-ear, I peek into the little oven window at the dollops of chocolate chip cookie dough and already can taste the warm explosion of sugar in my mouth. The heralding part of this moment, however, is when I hear the familiar sounds and bars of theme music to "Rudolph The Red-Nosed Reindeer." This Christmas television special loved by so many children all over the world snags my heart, and when the memorable snowman voiced by Burl Ives begins to speak, I tear down the hallway, jumping and landing on the sofa into animated bliss. There, safe and warm inside our little home from the cold winter, I catch glimpses of the festive and colorful Christmas bulbs outside, blinking in through the icy frost on the window above the TV. My mom is close behind me with a plate of warm cookies, and as I settle into the comforting music and lyrics of the legendary sounds of "Rudolph," everything is right in the universe.

This perfect moment was the safe haven that carried me through many a dark period in my life. It was my special place to run back to and touch "the singing of angels," and a moment that I spent half of my life trying to re-create by placing building blocks of illusions one on top of the other. Like a dangling carrot just out of my reach, it was the *home* I longed for. A place I felt safe and loved, but much like quicksilver, it escaped my grasp each time I tried to catch it, leaving me very sad.

Perfect moments are good for reminiscing, but at some point we have to let go.

Chasing Shadows

"When you stop chasing the wrong things,
you give time for the right things to catch up."
~Lolly Daskal, @LollyDaskal, Twitter
(25 Dec 2013)

There is a Zen proverb that says, "We stand in our own shadow, and wonder why it's dark." I have chased many things, attempting to gain light while increasing only darkness. My logical brain told me that if I "just do this" I could recreate that perfect world or time left behind. All around me, the light waited, but I didn't recognize it because I was blinded by preconceived ideas about how the world *should* work. My own perfect moment, while attempting to provide a light in the darkness, actually became a cloud, in some cases darkening my horizon and any possible outcome.

While uncomfortable with the unknown, sometimes it becomes easier to fill voids with feel-good memories, especially when we have experienced pain in the past. Not wanting to go there again, we create shadows, searching for our perfect moment in habits, rituals, relationships, or material things, desperate for anything that will bring us that good feeling once again. The downside is that these substitutes and illusions can cast darkness on the true spirit of who we really are, and if we are not careful, the distance back to *us*, to find our true spirit, can be a long way to travel. Ultimately, we waste time and energy chasing what is not real, while growing into something we are not, making it difficult to find out who it is we really are.

A good reality check is to ask ourselves if we are sacrificing reality for a comfortable self-made identity, one that through our own step-by-step building feels safe versus feeling alive. Are we chasing an identity we've outgrown? It's easy to get trapped clinging to self-images and concepts that make us feel happy or accepted, but if we keep creating and chasing shadows, the light will never catch up to us and we will never move forward and grow. We again, will get stuck.

Whether it is a really good day that we are trying to re-live or some cherished moment from the past that made us feel safe, whole, free, and happy, we should ask, "Is what I'm trying to capture separating me from now? Am I losing the opportunity to learn and grow being everything I can be in this moment? Am I living in the shadows of the past or the light of the present?"

Memories are to be cherished, not worshiped. Although cherished for their wisdom, and some memories appreciated for their nostalgia, they should never become our *God*. The lessons we gain from our memories or experiences are valuable, they make our reality rich with knowledge, and when reviewed and let go, should give us the power to create a most abundant life, not hold us back.

> "Life is a process of becoming, a combination of states we have to go through. Where people fail is that they wish to elect a state and remain in it. This is a kind of death."
>
> ~Anais Nin, *D. H. Lawrence: An Unprofessional Study*

Second chapter questions:

What is your favorite moment?

How did your first moment make you feel?

Ask yourself what you are chasing and why? Is it who you are now?

Where are you stuck?

· CHAPTER THREE ·

Picking up the Pieces

"The art of living does not consist in pre-
serving and clinging to a particular mode
of happiness, but in allowing happiness to
change its form without being disappointed
by the change; happiness, like a child, must
be allowed to grow up."

~Charles Morgan

W e can also embellish our perfect moments, making them better than what
they are because it is too difficult to face
what is uncomfortable. Who wants to open the childhood closet with its monster-fears of the past versus
skipping down the street linked arm in arm with
happy memories instead? Meanwhile, our insecurities
and denials lay buried, waiting to seize us in our life
choices, their repetition slowly constructing walls
around us, brick by brick. Wondering why our life

isn't working anymore, we point the finger at our outer circumstances and blame them for the way things are. This only encourages us to keep on chasing our perfect moment while living in the shadows.

When reviewing our past, all pieces are equally important, not just the fun, warm, fuzzy, or perfect moments. Every piece is important when putting it all together. Like a giant jigsaw puzzle of our life, the pieces have to fit. If we leave some pieces out or try to change them and make them fit, we won't have a clear picture of who we are.

Romancing our past distracts us from the more un-attractive and mundane moments that have tried to get our attention. These are the little gems whose brilliance have been lost and taken for granted because they did not wine and dine our senses. These were not, or are not, the moments that propel us out of bed with joy in the morning, but are instead the ones that pay the bills and deal with people and relationships challenging us in various ways; they were, or are, the real-life teachers. While these ordinary experiences may seem minuscule enough to fit into our back pocket, they are big with lessons and wisdom. While we don't always give these life-changing moments much thought, we should, because they are the underlying thoughts, and some-times grumblings, that skim just beneath the surface of our conscious thought. These minuscule moments have the same profound ability to bring us awareness and growth, even though they may not be covered in lollipops and roses.

While we may cling to happiness to avoid what we think will make us unhappy, the unhappy times can be just what we need to sustain long term happiness. They can mature us with a better understanding for the present, and at some point, our emotions have to have a chance to grow up.

The Perfect Life?

"All I wanted was a little piece of life, to be married, to have children . . . I was trying my damnedest to tend to a conventional life, for that was how I was brought up, and it was what my husband wanted of me. But one can't build little white picket fences to keep the nightmares out."

~Anne Sexton, interview in *Paris Review* (1967)

When we begin to re-evaluate and unravel our thoughts, we begin to unleash a barrage of questions. We release old feelings and rethink old values. We don't have to lose our cherished beliefs, but instead check ourselves by asking whether these ways of thinking produce fruit and open our heart. It is the heart that leads us to our soul. Without a change of heart, the head alone will never get you to your soul.

Are the stories you tell yourself—or someone has told you—about who you are and the blueprints you have designed for your life truly expressing who you are? Without the courage to face yourself and make these necessary changes, you will not reach your authentic self and life.

In our hurry to want something so badly, or what we think we want, it's easy to overlook everything to get it.

In Dr. Steven L. Hairfield's book, *A Metaphysical Interpretation of the Bible*, he wrote, "We have turned our minds away from Truth, thus shielding our hearts from the deeper experience of Christ Consciousness." Regardless of our beliefs, the point is we don't want to feel any more pain so we tell ourselves what we must to avoid it, yet without experiencing the truth we will never gain the depth of heart we need to forgive, truly love, and be our most genuine self. Whether there are too many painful memories to remember or we are lost in traditional ideas, or chasing our perfect moments, we have forgotten how and where to look.

Clinging to a moment, idea, identity, or possessions and holding on to a false sense of security for the sake of happiness, stifles the many changes needed for our growth. In turn, this bars the universe from expanding you into something extraordinary. Is your way of thinking the very obstacle that is blocking your path? The road that you may need to take, while not smooth and perfectly paved, and most likely filled with uncomfortable bumps, changes, and challenges, leads to the milestones that mark our journey. It is the learned strength from within these challenges that sets the wheels in motion and moves us forward to our own particular place. Without them, we live our Stepford lives behind the perfect white picket fences.

Facing the Boogeyman

> "Beliefs have the power to create and the power to destroy. Human beings have the awesome ability to take any experience of their lives and create a meaning that disempowers them or one that can literally save their lives."
>
> ~Tony Robbins, *Awaken the Giant Within* (1992)

I can sweep the pieces of my life, whether good ("Rudolph," marriage, family) or bad (abuse, a broken home, divorce) under the rug where they will hum for years beneath the surface, or I can face them, integrate them, and allow them to bring greater clarity and understanding to my existence.

Not all pieces are ones I like to remember, but if I don't go near them because it's painful, I miss the understanding and the meaning they bring to my life. Once I can get past the hurt, frustration, and even the joy, I am filled with a deeper understanding for the role I played on this particular stage and why. The whys do not always come easily, especially when traveling through pain. But navigating through these deep potholes in the road are necessary in order to find the lesson that waits at the end. It is what I walk away with that counts.

Like all unexamined pieces of life, these challenges form blind spots, spots that if not processed and learned from the first time will repeat over and over until, hopefully, we finally get it. Painful and devastating as they can sometimes be, these pieces are the debris in our lives that makes us stumble or the keys that can set us free. We can't move forward with heavy chains on our feet. We can't complete what the soul yearns for if blocked by feelings and emotions that we have not dealt with yet. What we believe and the choices we make will repeatedly reflect this. It's not easy to answer whether or not you have made friends with every aspect and part of yourself. This is why the path to authenticity is a narrow one and much of the time an avoided one. We grasp for things that make us happy, recreating and building tangible block on tangible block to get the good feeling of the first moment versus taking the time to feel our pain, or awkwardness, and restructure our life in a way that allows us to genuinely partner with our soul in real day-to-day life. Again in the wise words of Dr. Stephen Hairfield, "We have allowed our minds to lead us to this conclusion, merely because these 'things' are touchable and the soul is not—nor are the energies in life." To listen to the needs of our soul usually does not fit into our immediate plans or schemes and the results are not quickly as visible in our "instant-gratification" world.

The boogeyman is not someone or something we want to dwell on forever, but is certainly a part of our childhood or past that has to be faced. Until then, in the dark corners it holds captive our dreams that ebb and flow throughout our lifetime, disempowering us. Our callings are dampened by belief systems that make us choose over and over again the very choices that hold us back. You have the power to face, feel, and understand those fragments and pieces left behind. Don't be surprised if the old ideas about you begin to fall away. You may shake things up a bit but like the colorful pieces inside a kaleidoscope, every time your life is shaken up there are colorful new patterns that emerge. Within that colorful chaos you can begin to see a whole new you.

Give way to the Artist

"We are afraid of losing what we have, whether it's our life or our possessions and property. But this fear evaporates when we understand that our life stories and the history of the world were written by the same hand."

~Paulo Coelho, *The Alchemist*

As we begin to shed our old skin, slowly realizing a possible role in something greater, it can be easy to overlook the necessary trees ahead for the forest we are still trying to get to.

Just because we have had an epiphany does not mean that all life will cease as we know it with no more bumps in the road. When life has pulled out a rug from beneath us of everything we thought we were so sure of, the hurt and frustration does not just disappear overnight. Emotions have to be dealt with and a balance restored.

Regardless of their appeal (or lack thereof), we have to continue to embrace *all* moments if we are to grow. We chose these paths for a reason. While the lure of the new life is there, the old life patterns can return if we don't deal with them. We can choose once again to chase our perfect moments or hide in our cocoons of safety, running from our not-so-perfect moments, but sadly, neither choice allows the divine sculpting and chiseling needed to fully create our character, the character we are going to need for our new life. The chips may fly and the tears may fall, but until we deal with the denial, outdated beliefs, nightmares, fears, and other pieces of self, our spirit will never fly forward towards that greater forest.

Again, those defining moments and our experiences—as wild, profound or minuscule, nostalgic, crazy, or earth shattering as they may be—paint the story of us. The moments are pieces of us and a part of our life. In some cases we may not understand these moments right away, but life has a way of inevitably showing us what we need to see— if we stand back and let it. After we have extracted all the juiciness out of it, the past is dead. We need to let go and remember that the same hand that has painted our journey so far, still continues to be there painting our life, and through it all encouraging us with love and insight, while offering us the necessary tools for our new creation. However, sometimes rather than simply fixing it, we have to trust in the graces of the universe to show us how. When we get too busy trying to hold on and putting everything mentally or physically in its place, so careful not to fail, we lose out on the spontaneity of life and the marvelous little things that *just happen*. Sometimes it is in those accidents in life, beyond our control, that we are swept into realms of new possibility.

In Julia Cameron's book, *Walking in this World*, she reminds us of this with her advice to "wriggle out of the seriousness of rigid categorization and pursue the Pied Piper of delight." By letting the stars delight us, the moon whisper in our ears, or the rains refresh us, we reconnect *with the heavens*, but more so, we begin to hear our soul speak and feel our authenticity begin to move us. It will show us the way when our logic will not.

We have to be brave and trust that the artist knows what it is doing.

    "I don't see much sense in that," said Rabbit.

    "No," said Pooh humbly, "there isn't. But there was going to be when I began it. It's just that something happened to it along the way."

~A. A. Milne, The House at Pooh Corner

Third Chapter questions:

What is your least favorite moment? Have you faced it or run from it?

What are you holding on to?

What are your beliefs or values? Why?

· CHAPTER FOUR ·

Releasing the Secret

"Somewhere deep down in us is stored
the secret, and when we are digging in the
wrong place, we know it. The secret wants to
be discovered and will not let us go in peace
a way that is not ours."

~Elizabeth O'Conner

We can dig all our lives for the answers, for the secret we hold, but until we consider that we may not be digging in the right place, involved and too busy chasing perfect moments, we may never find them. It is evident by so many frazzled lives in our world today that we are not living genuinely or are disturbed. We hide ourselves, and then look desperately for ways to express ourselves that are not genuine. We cannot keep up the facade forever. It will catch up to us in unpleasant ways. In the timeless words of Lao Tzu, "He who knows others is wise. He who knows himself is enlightened." He knew that it is all of our *stuff*, whether mentally or physically, that keeps us from knowing and having a genuine relationship with our selves.

In an attempt to know yourself, it is important to start with the question, "If I was truly blossoming and flourishing in my life, what would my life look like?" When you begin to ask these types of heartfelt questions, you can trust that there is a creative hand putting a pen to your life that will write in people and events you could not have imagined. Shovel in hand, you begin digging in the right places all because you said "yes" to your heart.

We will not have peace with our self until we answer that voice that cries from within. More often than not, we take that calling for granted or deem it silly, all to continue digging in the wrong place until our haunting dissatisfaction becomes too great, forcing us to re-evaluate our life again and again. In order to change, we have to give the needed internal permission to our soul for creativity to take the helm. Fortunately, God does not give up on us so easily, placing the necessary bumps along our paths designed to wake us up and heed the call.

So around and around we go, back and forth, struggling with our illusions and ideas about what we should be doing or where we should be digging. When all along a simple small voice is tickling our ears and tugging our heart with divine guidance, trying to get our attention and waiting for us to answer. Bumbling along, we pick at life here and there, but when we hear the voice and begin to seriously dig with gusto, hitting that vein of gold and releasing our secret passion and purpose, our lives will never be the same. The richness of joy we set free and the appreciation of all that life has to offer elevates us from a life of a human being having a spiritual experience to a spiritual being having a human experience.

However, hiking the road back from not-so-perfect and difficult circumstances and taking that first leap can be difficult. We know we want a better life but are often too afraid to leave the known and well-worn path.

Trusting the Journey

> "No heart has ever suffered when it goes in search of its dreams, because every second of the search is an encounter with God and with eternity."
>
> ~Paulo Coelho, *The Alchemist*

Building or rebuilding your life and establishing a secure faith in where you're going, wherever that may be, means traveling through your insecurities and testing the waters here and there until eventually you feel courageous enough to dive in. With an open heart, your soul can finally step in, and stirring the energies, create experiences that can heal and balance you. Resting in the source that created you and sensing a new peace, you are now ready to become what God created you to be.

As you unwind and undo the many false beliefs and concepts that you have chased long and hard for happiness, it is time to step out into the void with trust. It takes a lot of courage to let go of the familiar and secure feelings, and embrace new territory. However, while stepping into the unknown may seem scary, there is more safety in striking out into new and exciting adventures that are *real*, verses living a life that is *unreal* and seemingly safe. No false foundation will hold you forever, and until you make up your mind to change, you will teeter on the fence of uncertainty. It is there that you toy with your dreams and your callings, fearing the possible outcomes of the choices you will make. You question, "If only you knew for certain." What you can know for certain is that clinging to the fence you will become stuck. Every choice we make, regardless of the outcome, is an encounter with God, and the only way we can move forward.

When I teach classes on Mindfulness or Meditation, I like to refer to the "chakras," or spiritual energy centers in the body, as a way to help participants visualize and understand how, when we decide to stay stuck in a mindset or a fear-based reality, it is like a pool of stagnate water. Past events or the resulting negativity we experience are stored in our energy centers or what is referred to as chakras. If we don't deal with this energy it can become trapped over time, making us feel emotionally and physically sluggish and bogged down, possibly leading to *dis-ease*. We have to deal with it. Similar to a blocked dam, no new energy can get through, and all kinds of emotional and past debris accumulates, only to increase our *dis-easement* or dissatisfaction. We have to release this negativity or something will do it for us. We either take initiative and make changes in our life, or we let our circumstances bring about those experiences that will pull the rug out from underneath us. Sometimes, in hindsight, we realize that while an experience may have been devastating, it is what we needed to shake us off the fence, and wake us up.

If we've dammed up all our emotions, closing doors and unwilling to take chances, how can the universe slip in and call us to something greater? When we hold on too tightly to our little known worlds for fear of a new outcome, we stifle our self and the energies around us. We were designed and created to swim in the waters of life, not sit on the shores. Granted, we may fear swimming to the other side because of deep water, but standing in the shallow stream, wading there for the rest of your life, can be a slow death as well. The tides have to be free to come and go, or life will not happen.

Fearing the common misconception that we are a loser if we fail, it becomes easier not to try. The only time we lose is when we don't act. We will always win when we act genuinely, moving towards what our intuition tells us, and listening to our secret. Trusting in our self and believing in our self, we come closer to God through succeeding or not. Knowing this, we can move on with a certainty that no matter where we wind up it is where we need to be at that moment for our greatest leap forward.

Breaking the Barriers

> "The moment a little boy or girl is concerned with which is a blue jay and which is a sparrow no longer can they see the birds or hear them sing."
>
> ~Eric Berne, Psychiatrist

It is easy to get lost in our labels of everything. We lose sight of the original backdrops of beauty or messages that speak to our heart. Preoccupied with our stories, or worried about outcomes, our concerns numb us and block our ears from the secret our soul whispers to us in each moment. Opportunities get left behind, as our authenticity comes second to our concerns. Our ears deaf, our eyes blind, our energy robbed, our hearts get tired. The freshness of life fades behind the dullness of repetition. A tree is simply a tree verses the strength and beauty it represents. A bird is simply a bird, rather than a gift of sweet melody or the marvel and freedom of flight. We forget how to see, hear, touch, smell, taste, and how to just be. We think and expect our life to happen or come to us in a certain way rather than appreciating it in the moment for what it is, whatever that form may be. We feel safe labeling and trying to control outcomes verses just letting things happen.

By releasing all that we hold dear, we do not lose that which is precious to us, but instead make way for spontaneity to offer us more. Separating ourselves from our hearts, out of feelings of fear, and selecting our moment to live in, our secrets never reach the surface. They are never released, and are never recognized for what they are, our passion. We dig our holes deeper without experiencing a deeper appreciation for what is around us. To see the blue jay or sparrow sing, we must return to a purity of heart, live in the spirit of unconditional love, and abandon the judging mind.

Digging in the right place is experiencing the depth of every experience of the universe rather than those select pieces of your life that you play over and over. Denials, and holding on to reframed moments to sustain you, will only haunt you later. They are the barriers that keep you from enriching your life with the *now* moments. Life is alive and all around you, moving with you and through you in synchronicity. To fully appreciate this, you have to dig where your heart guides you. Releasing your secrets, opening your heart and giving all you have to this moment, is the beginning of new creation, the new story that sits within you, ready to be told right now. Trust that in this moment you are right where you are for a reason and that some answers come in a guise you may not necessarily expect. They may be sitting on a branch or whispering in your ear, but trust that wherever they are, they will find you.

> "In our desire to impose form on the world and our lives we have lost the capacity to see the form that is already there; and in that lies not liberation but alienation, the cutting off from things as they really are."
>
> ~Colin Gunton

Chapter 4 questions:

What "secret" do you need to release for yourself?

What areas do you not trust about yourself?

What is holding you back from your passion? In your career or personally?

CHAPTER FIVE

Thriving Where You Are

"Your present circumstances don't determine where you can go; they merely determine where you start."

~Nido Qubein

Walking down the street one day, I came upon some bluebonnets growing through the cracks in the sidewalk. A few feet away was a garden full of them. What I found interesting was that the bluebonnets growing through the cement cracks seemed more robust, more vibrant, and more alive. They thrived, regardless of the heavy cement and tight cracks. Maybe these challenges are what forced them to strive harder, thriving, regardless of circumstances.

When we move forward, when we really make up our minds to do what is in our hearts, we push forth and something akin to pulling the cord on a parachute happens inside of us. A rush of energy suddenly lifts us up to heights we never expected. We blossom and bloom in a frenzy. No challenges, no barriers, no cement or tight cracks are going to stop us.

Once we have discovered our newfound wings, sometimes we have to keep digging to see where our feet of clay might still be currently stuck, and why. We can struggle to shift and change our external circumstances all day long, but until we free ourselves of our internally made traps, stuck in the mud and mire, we cannot fly. As Abraham Verghese writes so eloquently in his book, *Cutting For Stone*, we can set out on our journey and become masters of our ships, but when we look down, do we still see the "ancient, tarred, and mud-stained slippers" still stuck on our feet?

A Crack in the Egg

> "Not everything that is faced can be changed. But nothing can be changed until it is faced."
>
> ~James Baldwin, from the documentary
> *I Am Not Your Negro*

When the universe taps on our shell and we get a glimpse of what is calling to us through the crack, it's hard to go back to our humdrum life. However, and unfortunately for many of us, that is exactly what happens. "Oh, it sounded like a good idea, but ..."

Suddenly a mirror of our day to day life appears, and if the reflection and reality that we see does not fulfill the vision we want, we assume it wasn't meant to be. There, trapped within the mirror, are the roles, identities, and responsibilities that are part of us, day in and day out. Like an actor or actress, we run through the same script over and over in our heads, telling ourselves what we need to do or what we should be doing; the inner dialogue keeping those tarred and mud-stained slippers hard and fast around our feet. We have to ask, and face, which responsibilities and commitments are legitimate, and which are part of the ongoing story we have come to believe about ourselves. Bound by these stories, and stuck in the clay, we cannot dance freely with our creativity, passion and vision. We cannot thrive. And again, so as not to cause too much trouble, we safely lock away our callings and intuitions in a nice, safe, out of reach place. We might still hear the occasional call of our soul, but for the most part, we resume our safe and humdrum life, while simply dismissing the universe with all its possibilities. Without trust, without faith in our own ability and power to thrive, a callus of fear begins to form over our hearts, as doubts slowly creep back in. We quickly reach for the safety of our cookie cutter worlds, the illusion of control giving us a false sense of retrieving our senses. The universe, feeling our reluctance, begins to recede, letting us flounder in our safety net while our dreams once again slip from our hands, retreating into the small dark corners of our hearts.

Outside the Box

> "Life moves towards correcting the im-
> balance of the mind that the development of
> logic has brought on."
>
> ~Joseph Chilton Pearce, *The Crack in the Cosmic Egg:*
> *New Constructs of Mind and Reality*

In our world of time and linear thinking, we give ourselves options and solutions in a way that the universe does not. We see limitations as barriers. The truth is, the universe can take those limitations and turn them into opportunities that raise us far above any present challenges or circumstances. While we rely too much on our left brain to show us the way, our right brain begs to capture our heart with unlimited imagination. Life does have a way of correcting the imbalance that logic has brought on, and through our desire for a more meaningful life, once again, the universe will bring about whatever experience, to set that balance right. After rocking our world, and getting our attention, we may find that what we are left with is exactly what we need to thrive where we are. Usually, thinking outside the box frees us to receive answers through avenues we never dreamed, and is what keeps our dreams from slipping through our hands forever.

It takes courage to move out from behind a solely logical perspective on how life is supposed to work, and to listen to the far off call of your heart and soul. It takes moving in directions and ways we might not have considered before. The more years of logical conditioning, the more difficult it can be to lean on and trust a greater power, and right brain thinking, to show us new ways to blueprint our life. Relying on our inner resources to show us a different way may make us uncomfortable, but with every step and continued reassurance through the conviction of heart, we learn to trust that we have everything we need in this moment to live authentically, and with passion. This lets us know, regardless of current circumstances, we have what we need to start living our life in a way that brings us purpose right now. In fact, our circumstances, which may be tight cracks and a little cement, can bring us a resilience we never knew we had.

Carving the Niche

"It's important to understand that at every point of opposition to who we are or to what God has called us to do, we are presented with the options of either conforming and giving in, or standing our ground and becoming stronger in who God has made us to be."

~Constance Rhodes, *The Art of Being: Reflections on the Beauty and the Risk of Embracing Who We Are*

Creativity often makes us think of painting, writing, pottery, songwriting, etc. What about the art of daily living? We want to answer our calling but fear doing so. Why? What is it that we really want and what does that look like? How do we stay true to our passion? Being tethered to a life just to pay the bills or make others happy is not genuine joy. Carving out a niche in this life that makes our heart sing is joy. To get there we have to learn the art of daily living.

On the big seesaw of life, we balance precariously each day between what makes us happy and what we must do to live. We must be able to make peace in the battle between our conscious mind and our unconscious mind. If we can learn to teeter between life responsibilities and spirituality and calling, our masterpiece is in the throes of creation. However, before a painter can paint, he or she must decide what it is they are going to paint. We often have an idea of what we want in our lives but do not take the time to visualize or appreciate what this will look like, or what small changes we can make now. We can't change what we don't know needs to be changed. Without truly knowing ourselves, or a practical assessment, our canvases remains blank.

Your strengths and your weaknesses will determine what is on your canvas. What is your passion? How does your lifestyle fit in with this passion? How much time do you need to answer your calling: a day, a week, a month? What can you do differently in your job, your home life, or for your family? Carving out time for you, and standing strong in the face of adversity, is paramount in painting your pending dreams.

Our calling challenges us to thrive, like those bluebonnets in the sidewalk. Their passion for life and to grow helps them defeat the odds of their circumstances. They are flowers and are called to bloom. We are spiritual beings also called for a purpose. When you begin to ask yourself what that purpose is, and begin to live that passion each day, your life will arrange itself to meet your needs. Only when you begin to live that purpose in some small way by taking some small step towards action can the universe answer.

Thriving in our present circumstances, and being the best we can be, can teach us much. While our current circumstances may not be our choice of what or how we envision our purpose, we just may be at the cusp of what we need to learn in order to reach our next level. That leap of growth is just enough to push us forward. As we peer through the crack longing for our dreams and personal meanings, listening to what God has called us to do, our circumstances suddenly begin to change and to accommodate where the soul is taking us.

"Asking the proper question is the central action of transformation. Questions are the key that causes the secret doors of the psyche (and heart) to swing open." (Emphasis, author's)

~Clarissa Pinkola Estes, *Women Who Run With the Wolves: Myths and Stories of the Wild Woman Archetype*

Chapter 5 Questions:

What tools do you have right now and what is in your power to change?

What is real for you and what is not?

What are some changes you can make now, this week, this month, to get closer to your dreams?

• CHAPTER SIX •

A Walk Between Two Realms

"Every positive change—every jump to a higher level of energy and awareness—involves a rite of passage. Each time to ascend to a higher rung on the ladder of personal evolution, we must go through a period of discomfort, of initiation. I have never found an exception."

~Dan Millman, *Peaceful Warrior*

Walking down life's path is not always easy, and from time to time most of us will feel the pull and tug between our inner and outer worlds—the inner world where the *real* us waits, and the outer world that sometimes insists on a different face. It is at this point that our balance—spiritually, emotionally, and physically—becomes challenged, but necessary to get us over our hurdles and towards our desired destination. Our evolution must involve finding ways to restore that balance, bringing peace and healing to the inner conflicts that keep us from deepening our relationship with our true self, and openly expressing who we really are. We need time to reflect and develop clarity in regards to our relationship with our self and everyone and everything around us. We need to know what we are willing to compromise on, and what we are not, as we reach for a higher awareness.

Establishing a sense of balance that reflects our natural and uncompromising boundaries sets us free. Upon this achievement, we realize nothing or no one can impose their version of truth upon us, and our life is ours to do with what we will. Our higher power, that higher energy, recognizing this positive *realignment*, acquiesces to what is deeply within our hearts. Without the filters, we are able to look at our life and interpret our experiences in a way that empowers us to be able to choose what is really important to us.

You Make the Call

> "When we meet real tragedy in life, we can react in two ways—either by losing hope and falling into self-destructive habits, or by using the challenge to find our inner strength."
>
> ~Dalai Lama XIV

As our seesaw teeters this way and that, it is easy to see that keeping it perfectly balanced is not something we can always control; there will be events that threaten to throw that balance off and we have to be ready to face those challenges. Fortunately, we have the power in how we perceive our experiences, and the choices we make will determine just how far off that balance may or may not be.

When we deny our ability to be present with our experiences, we lose the opportunity to rise above and learn how to cultivate our inner strength. We lose our ability to communicate and confirm what we want from others and our environment. We either close down, or we accept and learn from our experiences, integrating the trials and using the wisdom to open ourselves to the next chapter of life. Only by keeping open and allowing ourselves to react—from a level of truth inside of us and feeling our emotions—are we free to monitor our reactions, and understand what makes us tick. In order to change, we have to be willing to be with ourselves. If we do not have a serious change of heart, or make some soul wrenching turns, we can easily fall back into old patterns and ways of thinking. The only way to our inner power is by being real to ourselves and others and by not compromising our true self. So why do we not always give ourselves permission to explore the full range of our emotions and feelings?

Discovering our emotions and feelings puts us in touch with the core of our beliefs and helps us to recognize self-imposed limitations. The more we expose our patterns of entanglement and traps we have laid for ourselves, the more aware we can become as to why we hide in our perfect moments. If being unrealistic and *fitting in* is more comfortable for us, then we will never fully experience our genuineness, or appreciate our life and the beauty, reward, and fulfillment available to us.

Our destructive habits and modes of thinking may be a quick fix and false salve for the pain, but long term, it will destroy our soul. We will paralyze our *self* from ever feeling our soul's needs and being able to express its yearnings and passion for life. We will lose whatever hope we have, and we will never fulfill or reach our callings.

Uncaging the Heart

"Your body is free but your heart is in prison. To release your heart, you simply reverse the process which locked it up. First you begin to listen for messages from your heart—messages you may have been ignoring since childhood. Next you must take the daring risky step of expressing your heart in the outside world... As you learn to live by heart, every choice you make will become another way of telling your story... It is the way you were meant to exist. If you stop and listen, you'll realize that your heart has been telling you so all along."

~Martha Beck, http://marthabeck.com/

The healed heart, like an open portal to the divine, allows us to freely remember the experience of our first moment. If the portal is closed, we forget how to remember. What did it feel like when we first encountered the divine? Where did that part of us go? Is it still there waiting for us to reconnect with it? Your heart can bring these questions into the light with answers that your mind alone cannot. Understanding this, is the first real step towards true healing. When you recognize the heart-messages that speak to you, and not the stories that your head is telling you, this truth—and ultimately this freedom—allows your life to reassemble itself in ways that are positively unimaginable. It is the groundwork for dreams and callings to follow. This truth acts as the magnet to bring our inner world and our outer world together, merging the two into one with astounding results. The risk of trying to hide behind our fears is far greater than exposing our hearts for what they really are.

"For the gate is narrow and the way is hard that leads to life, and those who find it are few."

~Matthew 7:14 (ESV)

There are many people who want a different life, but do not want to be accountable or take the necessary steps to change their life. Making hard decisions that take us out of our comfort zone is not appealing, but it is part of the rite of passage. This necessary honesty with ourselves and moving through our trials is what places our feet on the next rung of the ladder. It takes heart, and like working a muscle that is in jeopardy of atrophying if we don't work it, we risk losing our ability to hear and act upon what our heart is telling us, if we don't follow it.

With stories we have listened to for so long, and the tug of the perfect moment all too familiar, it is so easy to fall into a sense of security and complacency, telling ourselves that to reach for anything else would be too difficult. Martin Luther wrote, "Whatever your heart clings to and confides in, that is really your God." If our conceptions are confused, we worship gods that are popular or comfortable, ones that offer no real meaning. Not everyone is prepared or willing to challenge their inner demons and false gods, but those who do find themselves in a whole new relationship with life. One that, while not free of struggles, will reveal to us how we can use the tools of strife or pain, to develop internal resources that realize and define our ultimate purpose. The gate is open, our heart is speaking, are we ready to listen?

"Pocketfuls of Bliss"

"When I was 5 years old, my mother always told me that happiness was the key to life. When I went to school, they asked me what I wanted to be when I grew up. I wrote down "happy." They told me I didn't understand the assignment, and I told them they didn't understand life."

~John Lennon

In a world sometimes way too serious, we have to find the little things that make us smile. Waking up each day and exploring our life for laughter and a sense of joy and lightheartedness, frees up the universe to laugh with us. We must look for the *pocketfuls of bliss* to bring the gift of childlike carelessness back into our world.

The glimmers and glee of our first moment can fade quickly depending on our indoctrination into our world. Our divine sparkle is at risk with the loss of luminosity with each experience we encounter. That is why it is important for us to protect our inner light and let it shine at all costs. One of the ways to keep our light shining is to indulge in a little silliness now and then. Determined to live a life that encompasses happiness and enjoyment of what we do, is paramount to our life balance. Little pocketfuls of bliss can also keep us moving forward when things get tough. Sometimes though, throughout life experiences, we forget how to laugh or are fearful we will look out of place, or some events leave us feeling temporarily hopeless and threaten to steal our joy.

I remember such an event on my very first day of school. I was so excited to make a new friend. So, as luck would have it, after lunch at recess, I discovered a little girl in the same grade as me. Looking somewhat small for her age, I decided she looked like she needed someone to protect her. With a wide, open heart and excitement spewing forth all over the place, I ran up to her, eager and ready to be friends! I told her my name, how many pets I had, my favorite color, what I liked to do, and on and on. Well, she ran from me, scared, and, I assume, overwhelmed with my overzealousness to be friends. Thinking she might fall or hurt herself, I tried to catch her. Unfortunately, this made her run even harder from me, and she started to cry. The other kids on the playground became mad at me for scaring her, and so they started to tease me, and make fun of me. What started as such a sweet and simple thing turned into total disaster. Devastated and confused, I felt alone, embarrassed, and stupid. I felt like an ugly monster for upsetting this poor little girl. At the end of the day, I fell into my mom's arms, teary-eyed and scared, and vowing never to return to the first grade.

She explained to me, in the most loving and simple way, how maybe I should take things a little slower. She explained how each person was different, and how I shouldn't feel bad. I listened to my mother, but inside I was secretly vowing to never get myself in that situation again. I remember how I lost my first little piece of glimmer that day. My light still shined, but now I felt I had to be careful. With an internal guard now stationed at the parameters of my heart, I felt I couldn't just run willy-nilly, fully expressing how I felt. While not the most traumatic or devastating experience, for me, it was certainly one of the first experiences that was filed away.

But, if we are not careful, for each filed away experience, small or big, for each judgment or harsh criticism, we can lose a piece of our light, a cherished piece of us. In this big old world we learn pretty quickly from an early age what hurts and what doesn't. Sometimes it scares us to bring that light back out in to the open for whatever reason. Whatever feeling it may be, it is certainly a vulnerability we are not too eager to share again. We lose the ease of how to simply be happy and silly. The seesaw dips with fear as our carefree spontaneity subsides leaving us unbalanced. Without laughter, a sense of lightheartedness, or unconditional freedom of expression to keep our spirits soaring, life's burdens can get us down.

Pulling up the "Big-Boy Breeches"

> "Love is what we were born with. Fear is
> what we learned here. The spiritual journey is
> the relinquishment, or unlearning, of fear and
> the acceptance of love back into our hearts."
>
> ~Marianne Williamson, *Lighting the Lamp Within:*
> *Illumination the Path to Greater Spiritual Awareness*

Pulling up our big-boy (or girl) breeches means
bravely moving forward one step at a time with an open
heart, and discovering or rediscovering what makes you
grow while removing what doesn't. In every case, being
afraid to feel, take a risk, explore, love, or move forward
again will certainly tip the scale and throw off the balance. I once had a friend tell me, after I was lingering
in the dark too long, to pull up my big-boy breeches
and get moving again. Angry at first, I began to see she
was right. Scared to fail, with fear blocking me while I
developed a comfortable pattern of whining about the
unfairness of it all, her bold and straightforward words
hit home. A healthy dose of reality can do wonders.
Embracing life and throwing caution to the wind can
be terrifying when we are locked in the grip of our fears.
Sometimes it's easier to dance around the edges of our
life instead of fully jumping in and doing the tango, but
at some point our desire to dance must be greater, or we
shrivel up and die to the inner self.

Walking out into the world, and baring our heart on our sleeve, is a feat many people would just as soon cut off their right arm than do. The seesaw, heavy to one side with the weight and burden of past fears, misconceptions, and unhealthy filters, can keep us unbalanced and fearful of exposing our self to reality, and ultimately, love of self and others. Stuck on the ground, we never rise up to escape the gravity of our fears and the conditioned thinking that *this is all there is*. We cannot shine when our light is only turned on half way, but when turned on full force we are brilliant.

Losing our fears and pulling up our big-boy breeches does not mean trying to solve every problem right now. It does mean taking the first step into this moment and bravely facing our world, openly and willingly. It is accepting who and where we are right now today, and allowing love back into our hearts without judgment or fear. It means listening to our self, our heart messages, and letting our intuition guide us, giving us insight for whatever challenges we face, and most importantly, remembering why we are here.

Remembering the Mission

"When we feel passion for something, it is because we are remembering what it was that we came here to do. The more passion we feel, the more in alignment with Source we are, allowing this energy to pour through us with no hesitation. This is the way it was meant to be."

~Karen Bishop, *Remembering Your Soul Purpose*

When our life passion bubbles and ignites, it overshadows our grown-up fears and concerns. The logic and control we try to attach to our outer world moves over as the energy of our inner world breaks through the surface and makes itself known. We are lifted by the wings of our soul as it carries us high above worldly concerns and into the stream of consciousness and creativity. Once realigned with our inner resources, the confidence, balance, and ultimately peace that results from this connection, lets us know we are on the right path.

Combining the head and the heart begins to give our purpose a face, and provides us with new faith and hope to move forward with our life plans. When we take the time to see what our passion looks and feels like, the excitement can help us to uncover the courage necessary for the changes in our lives that can make our dreams and purpose real. We are now creating our destiny. If we feel our passion, not afraid to let our heart sing, clarity will finally swoop in to fill the void where fear and judgment have sat for so long. We release our self from the perfect moments that hold back our freedom to experience each moment in a new and expansive way. Through our rites of passages we wrestle with our weaknesses and our fears, while learning our strengths, abilities, and talents.

If we find the courage and dare to walk through that narrow gate, letting go and acknowledging who we are right now, and relate to our life on those terms, we arrive on the threshold of divine self, and a chance to create all we hope for.

"As our awareness begins to shift, old patterns are beginning to break down and we lose our familiar points of reference. We need to let go and flow with events, not knowing the outcome but trusting in divine purpose."

~June McLeod, *Colour Psychology Today*

Chapter 6 Questions:

What does your balance look like?

What is uncomfortable for you right now?

What are some ways you take time just for you?

Are you discovering yourself in new ways? How?

CHAPTER SEVEN

The Creative Soul

"If we fail to nourish our souls, they wither, and without soul, life ceases to have meaning... The creative process shrivels in the absence of continual dialogue with soul. And creativity is what makes life worth living."

~Richard Carlson and Benjamin Shield,
Handbook for the Soul

O ur first moment, that deep experience with the soul, bridged our inner and outer worlds, if only for that moment, in complete oneness. As children, we could often experience that connection. Simple, everyday miracles and *magic*, through our own wonder and creativity, were the glue that kept us connected to universal source and inspiration. The miracle and magic of song, paintings, fantasy, and imagination left an openness that surrounded us in infinite possibilities. We marveled at nature as it enfolded us within its beauty. For many of us, despite our circumstances, our hearts could be nourished and resilience abound, because we were free to imagine and create through our many mediums. Our souls were free to whisper to us the mysteries and meanings of life, our young hearts not questioning or trying to reason. At one with our world, we were free to create and be created.

As adults, creativity offers us a way to retrieve those lost pieces of self, and to reclaim the qualities associated with being young at heart and comfortable in our own skin. Like a bridge to the soul, it can keep us connected, nourished and whole, and like a child, we can stop and marvel at the world for a while.

Walking Across the Waters

> "If we go down into ourselves, we find that
> we possess exactly what we desire."
>
> ~Simone Weil, *The Just Balance*

When I write or journal, it forces me to go deep down into myself. I touch areas that don't always see the light of day, but yet float just beneath the surface. I never cease to be amazed at the source of inspiration and strength I find at those depths. It is there that I can walk across the waters of everyday life. Connecting me to greatness I cannot explain, it provides a way to nourish what I am aching for. Like a creative prayer, asking for what I desire and answering in ways I usually do not expect, writing captures what I hear from my soul, and helps me to reach the answers within. Writing gives me the medium to freely and comfortably express what I feel. When I am done, I feel refreshed, left with a faith and confidence I can only receive from this power within.

While I see God in the beauty all around me and I am most intimate with this power through creativity, it is the action that, for me, bridges my two worlds. Creativity calms my emotions, and usually provides insight to most of my frustration and confusion. It brings peace and it brings wholeness. For me, it helps me be a better person.

There are so many ways to bring our selves to the surface, but few people actually make the time or have an outlet to do it. Creativity is one way of plugging back in to our inner self. It offers us the intimacy to express ourselves, at our own comfortable pace, in a safe and comfortable environment. We may know what it is we want to create, but even if we don't, just the act of creating, bringing out some feeling from the depths of ourselves, is a way to lose control in a controlled world. It provides the temporary freedom necessary to explore, and to reflect, what's going on inside. It is an activity in which we can express ourselves openly and freely without judgment.

If we are looking for ways to nourish our souls and to cultivate meaning, creativity can meet that need. We may not be a Rembrandt or a Robert Frost, and that's okay. What matters is how we express our selves, and if we submit, creativity will reflect that deeper part of us, guiding us into places we do not readily explore. Helping us to let go, and interact with a different side of who we are, creativity frees us to see in new ways, and to release what it is beneath the surface.

In God's Image

> "There's no beauty that you could perceive
> or create if it were not already within you…"
>
> ~Peter Shepherd, *Daring to be Yourself*

I have heard people say, "I'm not creative. I can't draw anything." If you can appreciate any beauty in life, it is in you to be creative. You are not of this world; you may have been born here, but your origins dictate that you are far greater than the identity you have donned in this world. You were created with the potential to create, and in an image that was made for endless possibility. Creativity can provide you the platform to see with and through your child heart with adventure, and no adult barriers.

Using your creative expression, and the freedom it offers, gives you the okay to color outside the lines. You create what you want and how you want it. You have complete freedom, and have always had it. You should never hand over your freedom, or greatness, to someone or something that dictates what your freedom or greatness should look like. It is up to you to discover what your own unique beauty or image is, and creativity can open up a path for you to do just that. It can alleviate the sense of mundane by expanding our minds and hearts through more involvement with intuition and insight. As Einstein said, "The logical mind will take you from point A to B, but the imagination will take you everywhere." Creativity is a spiritual energy that can create anything you can imagine, while taking you to new heights within yourself.

Opening Your Eyes

"The only real voyage of discovery consists not in seeking new landscapes, but in having new eyes."

~Marcel Proust, *Remembrance of Things Past*
(paraphrase of text in Vol. 5-*The Prisoner*)

Does our world really keep changing or is it us who keep changing? Does running away from, or denying the past, really create a new life? We are the creators of our world, subject to events, different people, and different places, but ultimately what is in our hearts. No matter where we run, our heart will follow, healed or not—and determine what we create. Whether it will be new or the same old thing is determined by how we choose to see it, and if we are willing to make the necessary changes.

As the architects of our life, we determine how we will frame or build our life. Our tools of mind and heart create the cornerstone for what we will build. If we are angry and bitter, our world is angry and bitter. If we cannot forgive, or deny, a painful past, the foundation we build will never hold us. Try as we might, we cannot build a loving home in that way. The only way to *fix* the past is to discover who you are now. Our life is an ongoing story and a creative process, and what we have painted on our canvas today, will determine what was painted in the past, and in the future, and the stories we tell ourselves.

When we paint a picture, sew, or write, we look for colors, words, stitches, whatever it is that we need to create our masterpiece. We test the medium in different ways, trying this or that. We learn what works and what doesn't and we do it all from a place that is real, from a creative source. Then why would we choose to live our life any differently? Isn't it from a creative source also? Would we use the same stories, hurt, anger or judgment if we are recreating our self? We are colorful, and vibrant spiritual beings with gifts to offer our world. We just have to see ourselves in the real sense of who we are. If we don't know what that is, we need to find out.

Creation doesn't worry about status quo; it doesn't worry about what people might think of it. It just is. Therefore, we are free to create artistically, and free to create a life of meaning and purpose with new eyes and a change of heart, in any way that we want to, in any way that is real for us.

As we paint or write, our real self, just beneath the surface, waits to be understood and expressed, our brush or pen capturing what needs to be said. Our drawings, poems, paintings, and songs embrace what our heart needs to feel or remember. Through our new feelings and expressions we can look at the world from our soul more naturally. Life becomes more effortless, as the bridge between our life's purpose and our soul's code becomes more evident, without ever leaving our current landscape. Standing in the same world we always have, we are a new creation destined for a purpose. We don't have to leave the world to see how beautiful it is, we just have to change how we see it.

"The basic project of art is always to make the world whole and comprehensible, to restore it to us in all its glory and occasional nastiness, not through argument but through feeling, and then to close the gap between you and everything that is not you, and in this way pass from feeling to meaning."

~Robert Hughes, taken in part from a quote in
The Shock of the New

Chapter 7 questions:

What creative activities did you enjoy as a child?

What is the first step you can do to bring creativity in to your life?

What will your creative time alone look like?

What is keeping you from creating?

CHAPTER EIGHT

Gratitude

"The best and most beautiful things in
the world cannot be seen or even touched.
They must be felt with the heart."

~Helen Keller

Awareness, like an open door, invites us to
reality—while gently closing the door on
the things in our life that no longer matter.
What took me a while to recognize in my own life, is
that this awareness, not born of the head, but of the
heart, is what truly perpetuates ongoing healing. It
is only through the heart that the universe, or God,
can be felt, accepted, and truly appreciated. The mind
alone will always offer the temptation to divide and
fragment our universe, threatening and disturbing our
reality. It is the clarity and feeling of the heart that
brings wholeness to both.

A wounded and unappreciative heart that has closed itself off cannot appreciate the wonder and beauty that surrounds it; it cannot appreciate the higher power and wisdom that is enfolded within everything, until it can accept everything for what it is. Maybe forgiveness does not come right away, but at least acceptance puts us at the door to truth, and hopefully at some point, forgiveness. The more acceptance and gratitude we have for those experiences that teach us, the quicker we learn to reconnect with life, healing ourselves, and becoming more spiritually evolved and insightful beings.

Like Bees to Honey

> "The more you recognize the immense good within you, the more you magnetize immense good around you."
>
> ~Alan Cohen, (1954) American businessman

My grandma used to tell me that if I was a good little girl I would attract good things and people in my life "like bees to honey." She was right, but it took me a while to understand that it's not just the action of doing good that attracts, but the sincere appreciation of doing so.

Without recognizing that I have the capability of being a really good person, my acts of kindness are shallow. My immense goodness, is what makes my acts of kindness genuine. My appreciation for myself, others, and the love I feel in my heart is what makes kindness a sincere act. If I feel I am not worthy, acting out of some guilt or shame, or trying to *buy my way into heaven*, my kind acts are worthless. As long as I have limited acceptance and appreciation of myself, I cannot completely accept and appreciate others and my world around me. Without recognizing and appreciating that I am perfect as I am, I will never be good enough. But, if I know that I am all that I need to be in this moment, appreciating whatever it is that looks like, the universe responds to that thought, and the world around me reflects that thought through abundance, love, and forgiveness.

Why is it we critique ourselves so much more than we appreciate what and who we are? Appreciation is not what we see with the eye, but feel with the heart. The mind alone, through its judgments, will never truly appreciate us completely for who we are, telling us stories as to why we will never be good enough. In truth, we deserve to be happy, to have love, and to give love. We are not perfect, but yet, through the heart, will always be perfect enough in this moment as we are. Many dreams and callings sit up on a lofty shelf for this reason—waiting for us to be worthy enough, or for our situations perfect enough, whatever that may be. If we let ourselves succumb to this thinking, the timing will never be right. We will never be "good enough."

Breathe Easy

> "I have learned over a period of time to be almost unconsciously grateful—as a child is—for a sunny day, blue water, flowers in a vase, a tree turning red. I have learned to be glad at dawn and when the sky is dark. Only children and a few spiritually evolved people are born to feel gratitude as naturally as they breathe, without even thinking. Most of us come to it step by painful step, to discover that gratitude is a form of acceptance."
>
> ~Faith Baldwin

Accepting ourselves in this moment invites gratitude. It allows us to breathe easy, knowing it's okay to be who we are right now. *I'm good enough for whatever comes my way and can accomplish what I need to do. I can open up my heart and be okay.* When practicing this awareness—letting our heart speak to us in this moment each day with this simple truth—our fear and anxiety eventually diminish as appreciation is left in its place. With the growing recognition of all our blessings, and the brimming appreciation for whatever the moment holds, the heart attracts the like through each interaction. We breathe a little easier with the recognition that through our appreciation, we will always be given more, providing our heart is open and we are sincere.

No matter what comes our way, there is an opportunity to accept that this too will help us in some way become more enlightened. Our appreciation additionally helps us to trust in something greater than ourselves, with a faith that we are here for a reason, and it is through this understanding that the universe replies in amazing ways.

Unbound by worries of who we *should* be or who we were, we can appreciate who we are now and stop blaming ourselves for painful pasts. We can take what we have learned and build upon that knowledge, using it for good and expanding our relationships, careers, and purpose. We can believe and *know* that we are worth so much more than we have been telling ourselves. We can discover and appreciate others as well, honoring who they are right now, and releasing them from the stories we tell ourselves about them, instead holding them in our heart with compassion.

When we can greet each day and situation with appreciation, we become aware of the beauty and majesty in everything around us. We remember how to let the moonlight and the stars in the evening sky inspire us. We hear the birds as they wake us each morning. Our heart is reunited with all of life, and our mind follows with a new sense of wonder, encouraging ideas and creativity.

Appreciate what has been; it has made you who you are today. Use that insight. Start living the dreams that you feel passionate and purposeful about. Remember: no one can tell you differently except you.

> "You, yourself, as much as anybody in the entire universe deserve your love and affection."

> ~The Buddha

Chapter 8 Questions:

What are some insights into your life right now that can move you forward?

What are some ways you can appreciate yourself more?

What new things have you experienced that lead you closer to your life purpose?

• CHAPTER NINE •

Believe

"Faith is to believe what you do not see; the reward of this faith is to see what you believe."

~Saint Augustine

Ask yourself, repeatedly if necessary, what fills you—what moves you? Where do you pull strength from when you most need it? Swami Vivekananda said, "You cannot believe in God until you believe in yourself." If you don't know who you really are, or your core beliefs, out of an inability to contemplate what is within you, how can you believe and move forward? If the images you project about yourself are powerful enough to disconnect you from your true self, if they do not serve you genuinely, they are not real. So then, find what moves you, serves you, and believe this with all your heart. Protect it, it is precious, and know that faith is believing that anything is possible, and knowing this is true, is the reward of that faith.

Regardless of what we have believed, or what we believe in this moment, remembering and believing that we are never separate from the power that exists within us can keep us grounded, and in reality. Believing and holding on to what the heart knows, and ultimately what our soul yearns for, can give us the faith to change our lives to reveal not only what is yearned for, but is in actuality, a real part of our lives.

The Proverbial "Hooks"

> "I believe in God, but not as one thing, not as an old man in the sky. I believe that what people call God is something in all of us. I believe that what Jesus and Mohammed and Buddha and all the rest said was right. It's just that the translations have gone wrong."
>
> ~John Lennon

As previously mentioned, whatever we cling to is our God, any perfect moment—good or bad—is our "hook." Our minds, snagging these moments and weaving them into tapestries of beliefs, will translate them into what we want to see or believe, and that belief has the power to either create or destroy. We either expand or shrink, move forward or stall; it all depends on what we believe. The "old man in the sky" doesn't determine whether you follow your dreams or live your passion. The image you have created in your mind, with desire in your heart, is the propelling force that moves you forward and into action, whatever it may be. The God *within you* will call you towards your purpose; whether or not you decide to follow that call is up to you.

Gary Zukav, spiritual teacher and author, has said, "the longest journey is the one from the mind to the heart." Our belief systems are subject to our experiences. Those translations have the ability to bring people together, through compassion and love, or divide us. It is the long journey through unprocessed feelings, the healing through the heart that restores our sight, ultimately giving us clear perspective. Until then, our interpretation can destroy us daily if seen through unprocessed guilt, hurt, un-forgiveness, or pain, thwarting our efforts and attempts to touch a sincere reality. When we agree to change our life, when we agree to pick up the pieces of ourselves and re-examine them in a new and different light, accepting things as they are, we free up our minds to believe in who we are in this moment. We can begin to identify and believe in our passion, and ultimately why we are here, and begin to see it unfold.

The Ripple Effect

> "Everybody talks about wanting to change
> things and help and fix, but ultimately all you
> can do is fix yourself. And that's a lot. Because
> if you can fix yourself, it has a ripple effect."
>
> ~Rob Reiner

Everything we do affects everything and everyone around us. Our translations, our beliefs, are at the core and center of our world, and include others. Either we react from a wounded self or a healed self. Our beliefs determine our outcomes. Yet, the majority of us sit and complain about our situations. If we want to *fix* our world, we have to fix or change *us*. We have to be the one to undo what has been done. No one can do it for us. Having blindly followed the world that we have built and believed in, we have unknowingly enslaved our authenticity to our demands, compromising our hopes and dreams. The rough waves of our chaotic emotions, and negative views, ripple out into the world making us reap what we sow. Unfortunately, through those unresolved feelings, our purpose will not be realized, leaving us hopeless and unfulfilled.

If we want to see the world or our self in a better place, then we have to believe it and live it. When we believe that we are not broken, accepting ourselves with love and compassion, we will learn to see with love and compassion into the hearts of others. When we forgive our own humanness and frailty, and love our self for who we are, we will be able to unconditionally love others.

We are powerful beyond our beliefs. When we begin to trust and believe this, for there is no reason not to, we can confidently move forward with both heart and mind present and ready for action. Then and only then can we see the ripple effect of creation move our heaven and earth into one.

The Young at Heart

> "I try to believe like I believed when I was five...when your heart tells you everything you need to know."
>
> ~Lucy Liu

Waking up the heart to appreciate everything for what it is, doesn't have to be the difficult and complex journey we make it out to be. We look here and we look there for the truth, for *the key* or *the answer*, to our lives, when it hides in plain sight.

An interesting question is posed by Steven Hairfield in his book, *A Metaphysical Interpretation of the Bible*, "If you were the God in whom we all believe, and if you wanted to hide this most powerful key in such a way that any one of us could discover it, how would you go about it and where would you conceal the object?" He wrote that part of the answer lies in the words of the Bible when the Master told us, "to enter the kingdom of heaven we must have the mind and innocence of a child."

Regardless of our belief system, it is true that with a childlike heart, a heart not bound and closed by bitterness or past residuals, and free to love, we continue throughout our live to hear the heart-messages that speak to us. This intuition serves as key in our interactions with all of life. As adults, we look for an almighty powerful God, but yet, when we hear this power speak to us from within, we are not confident enough to hear and accept what it tells us. We lack the necessary faith in order to believe. Access to our spirituality is not out of reach in some "airy-fairy" far off realm, but lies within us, in the innocence and purity of a united heart and mind. The confusion of trying to find it in the opinions and the beliefs from the conditioning we grew up with not only prevent us from entering this kingdom, but may be why we made a wrong turn on the path to begin with.

The inherent *knowing*, the faith and belief of a child that everything *is as it is*, is not man-made, but a natural perspective from a stillness of mind and heart not yet disturbed.

Pay Attention

"The moment one gives close attention to anything, even a blade of grass, it becomes a mysterious, awesome, indescribably magnificent world in itself."

~Henry Miller

There is a richness of life that surpasses our understanding, all around us. Personal pain, hurt or loss is so unique to each person, that's why nature and creativity is such a powerful anecdote for healing. It reaches out to each person in their own way. I love the words of a woman by the name of Alexandria K. Trenfor: "The best teachers are those who show you where to look, but don't tell you what to see." Her quote allows us a rich meaning from several different perspectives.

The best teachers allow the subject to speak to our hearts freely without interpretation. Like instrumental music, we hear the beauty of the notes without any words to interpret a meaning for us. It leaves us to our own imagination and gives the universe a chance to rush in, filling the gap with indescribable beauty.

Like children being able to enter the kingdom of God, we may simply gaze upon the newness in each and every thing, therefore seeing the simple truth and wonder in most things, simply as they are.

Applying these principles to our self and our surroundings leave us in a position to be filled with possibilities. When we see with clarity the truth (rather than perfect moments) in everything, everyone, and in every experience, we invite inspiration and passion. The silent teachers rush in to build our character, cultivate compassion, and ignite our creativity while opening space in our hearts to believe in our self and what we can achieve. Then and only then can we view things clearly, with an attentiveness not full of judgment and clouded. Like a child, and with our own wisdom, we suddenly see that "mysterious, awesome, indescribably magnificent world in itself." It speaks to our heart with the answers and keys that we need.

Always Hear the Bell

> "At one time, most of my friends could hear the bell, but as years passed, it fell silent for all of them. Even Sarah found one Christmas that she could no longer hear its sweet sound. Though I've grown old, the bell still rings for me, as it does for all who truly believe."
>
> ~Chris Van Allensburg, *The Polar Express*

When I was little, we had a silver, aluminum Christmas tree with a color wheel. Each Christmas, I would sit in front of that tree for what seemed like hours just watching it turn from red, to blue, to green, and finally to yellow or gold. To enhance the effect, my father only decorated the tree with red, blue, silver, and gold glass balls. To me it was the most beautiful thing I had ever seen. There were reflections of a little distorted me in each ball. As I sat there and watched myself turn different colors, I remember a feeling like nothing on Earth. From some place deep inside me, my own sweet bell rang loudly, giving rise to an un-impenetrable belief in something, once again, so much more significant than my earthly self.

And now, years later, as I sit in my living room at Christmastime, cherishing the lights and ornaments, I let them transport me back to that special place once again. In the little glass balls I still see me, a little older, in different colors and with distortion. It reminds me that no matter what I have been through, that power, that source of inspiration, that exists in me is always there. It also reminds me that while I have been through distortion in my life and have transitioned through many colorful events, that power has made me stronger. I believe that whatever I can imagine, whatever I can dream and feel in my heart will, like a magnet, attract whatever it is that will make it real. I know, through faith, that tucked away in this universal soup made up of opportunities, lessons, people, and experiences, is exactly what my purpose calls for. I may not always understand the *why* and *how*, but can appreciate that there is something greater at work. And as long as I believe, God will answer in the most moving and powerful of ways.

Making up your mind to believe, choosing to gaze upon life with surrender and passion, and opening and baring your heart without fear will ring the bells, and when they begin to toll there is absolutely nothing to hold you back.

"The human spirit is stronger than anything that can happen to it."

~C. C. Scott

Chapter 9 Questions:

What do you believe in and what are your hooks?

Do you hear the sweet bell?

In what ways does your own greatness move you?

In what way have your beliefs changed over the years? Why?

CHAPTER TEN

This Present Moment (Rising Above)

"There is something in the human spirit that will survive and prevail, there is a tiny and brilliant light burning in the heart of man that will not go out no matter how dark the world becomes."

~Leo Tolstoy, *Wise Thoughts for Every Day: On God, Love, the Human Spirit and Living the Good Life*

We talk about the darkest moments stealing our light, but I have found throughout my life that sometimes it is in those dark and dreary moments that we find our light. Wherever you are in this moment, you are not alone and never in complete darkness. When forced into a corner, it is there, in that challenge, that we can choose to *rise above*. Using our inner resources, we have the wisdom to prevail, if we will listen to that inner voice. Whatever shadows the world may offer us can never compare to the voice of the authentic human spirit that continues to cry out. Listening to this inner greatness, and openly admitting to ourselves that we are lost, we find an inspiration so bright we need never fear the dark again. It is here, in our innocence, disrobed of any ego, beliefs or opinions, that our first moment is unveiled and with it the understanding that we never really left it.

The Way Home

> "When I've lost my way or when I'm confused about a path to take, I remember that most answers I need I already possess—deep inside. I am naturally creative, resourceful and whole. If I consult my invisible compass, I'll know what to do.
>
> ~Steve Goodier

Like the key that lies waiting for us, our answers are never that far away. Many times we are too stubborn to ask for help, but sometimes a simple statement or confirmation of faith, like "show me the way," can provide amazing results. Never truly lost, we always have the power to find our way.

For most of us, the first moment or divine encounter was easy. Like the kingdom of heaven for a child, our innocence held out an open invitation. The divine could reach us. As an adult, once again standing behind our opinions or traditional beliefs, many of us forgot what we originally possessed through our childlike innocence. We believe in, and prefer, our own abilities to simple faith.

Planning, scheming, organizing, and arranging life from a reaction, versus letting things happen naturally, I've had to ask myself, "How much room did I leave for the natural flow of things—for reality, for God?"

Being separated from our self is kind of like hide-and-seek. Most of us know what we are looking for, but from our limited perspectives or conditioning, the translations are all wrong. We don't know what *God* looks like, or we think we know what it is *supposed* to look like. Until we consult our invisible compass, and rely on our inner resources to guide us, we will miss how close God really is to us.

Cracking the Shell: Being Real with Yourself

"For a seed to achieve its greatest expression, it must come completely undone. The shell cracks, its insides come out and everything changes. To someone who doesn't understand growth, it would look like complete destruction."

~Cynthia Occelli, *Resurrecting Venus*

It's scary for most people to come *undone*, or admit that at some point they did come undone. However, sometimes it's the only way for the rubber to meet the road. Not a sign of weakness, not a sign of destruction, and not a sign that we are a dysfunctional or broken person, coming undone can be our greatest ally and achievement, flushing the *real* us up to the surface with an admission to ourselves that we are lost.

With an open crack, we can look in and see ourselves exposed, maybe for the first time. Old relationships or experiences from the past replay, to give us new insight and perspective. All of our denial and rejection sift out through the cracks, and throughout the chaos, and unexpected transformation, all that is left is bare truth.

As discussed in Chapter 3, whenever we are picking up pieces of our self, wherever they may lie, it is not easy. But if the heart and head are ever going to come together in blessed union, we need to be completely honest with our self, pinpointing our emotions, and searching for the origins of our beliefs and views. Our shell wide open now, we suddenly realize we are okay, as years of pain and frustration slip away. Aligning our heart with what we know to be real, and making eye contact with our self without the burdens of the past, gives us a clear glimpse of *home*, allowing us once again to dance with the Devine.

Reality: The Builder

"You never change things by fighting the existing reality. To change something, build a new model that makes the existing model obsolete."

~R. Buckminster Fuller

Whether hair-raising, hair-pulling, tearful, incredible, or miraculous, our experiences in life are the building blocks that force us to reinvent ourselves every day, in every moment. We can fight the change, or we can use our inner abilities and insight, and from them build a whole new world.

Whatever leftover ashes you find yourself sifting through, you can never rebuild the past. Rather than fight what we face, we can use our inner strength and resilience to redefine who we are, and where we go from here. When we experience our humanness from this perspective, we are fulfilling ourselves with the richness of our *sacred contract*. We find new ways of doing things, and new gifts and talents we didn't know we possessed. It is our change of heart and mind that will erect our dreams from the ashes of the past. Our purpose evident as our new model for living is constructed lesson by lesson, moment by moment.

It's what we do with each moment that counts. Moments do not come into our lives to hang onto forever or judge. They come to teach us, to develop us. Creatures of habit and control, we resist change. In doing so, we can miss the simple genius that exists in each moment.

Progress won't occur if it's confined in the mind set of *safe perspectives*, or what that progress should look like traditionally, individually or as a group. Progress has to be free to move forward. Demanding excellence and integrity and rising above our circumstances, while dedicated to seeing the moment with crystal clarity and compassion, is what will propel us forward. This is the difference between chasing the perfect moment and living in a moment that is alive with opportunity. It is the difference between existing and excelling, and the difference between holding on to the dreams whispered in our first moment, and actually unleashing them in our life now. This is our perfect moment.

> "What day is it?" asked Winnie the Pooh.
>
> "It's today," squeaked Piglet.
>
> "My favorite day," said Pooh.
>
> ~A. A. Milne, *The House at Pooh Corner*

.

About the Author

Ginny Brown is a certified life coach and community health worker. She has a background in business, marketing, and administration. Currently she is a program coordinator and instructor for a national nonprofit educational organization.

www.ingramcontent.com/pod-product-compliance
Lightning Source LLC
LaVergne TN
LVHW041159080426
835511LV00006B/671